WILD WICKED WONDERFUL

TOP 10:

PARTNERSHIPS

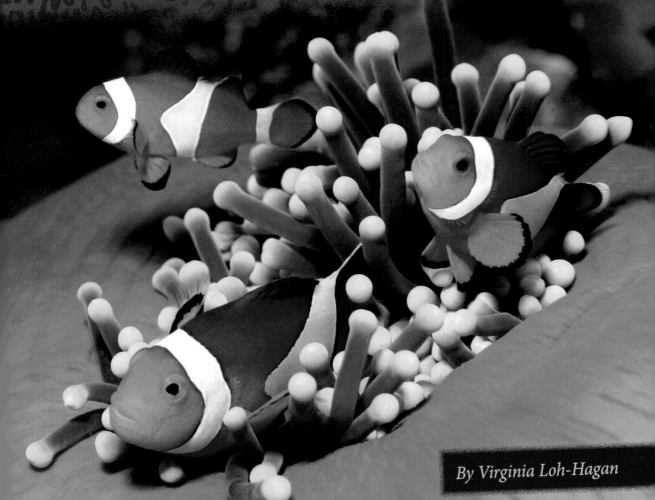

By Virginia Loh-Hagan

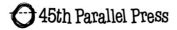
45th Parallel Press

Published in the United States of America by Cherry Lake Publishing
Ann Arbor, Michigan
www.cherrylakepublishing.com

Content Adviser: Stephen Ditchkoff, Professor of Wildlife Ecology and Management, Auburn University, Alabama
Reading Adviser: Marla Conn MS, Ed., Literacy specialist, Read-Ability, Inc.
Book Designer: Melinda Millward

Photo Credits: © Andaman/Shutterstock.com, cover, 1, 21; © Kitch Bain/Shutterstock.com, 5; ©Kasparart/Dreamstime.com, 6; ©NOAA/NMFS/SEFSC Pascagoula Laboratory; Collection of Brandi Noble, NOAA/NMFS/SEFSC/http://www.flickr.com/CC-BY-2.0, 6; © Nature Picture Library / Alamy Stock Photo, 7; © Norbert Wu/ Minden Pictures/Newscom, 8; © Moizhusein/Dreamstime.com, 10; © Artush/Shutterstock.com, 10; © Eric Isselee/Shutterstock.com, 10; © Suateracar/Dreamstime.com, 11; © Alta Oosthuizen/Shutterstock.com, 12; © SteveAllenPhoto/Thinkstock, 12; © Stephan Raats/Shutterstock.com, 12; © Jezbennett/Dreamstime.com, 13; © Mike Bauer/Shutterstock.com, 14; © Dai Mar Tamarack/Shutterstock.com, 14; © Marty Wakat/Shutterstock.com, 14, 15; © Dennis W Donohue/Shutterstock.com, 16; © Katherine McGovern/Shutterstock.com, 16; © aaltair/Shutterstock.com, 17; © Stuart G Porter/Shutterstock.com, 17; © Sainam51/Shutterstock.com, 18; © Moments_by_Mullineux/Thinkstock, 18; © FLPA / Alamy Stock Photo, 19; © Ewan Chesser/Shutterstock.com, 19; © Joze Maucec/Shutterstock.com, 20; © cbpix/Shutterstock.com, 20; © feathercollector/Shutterstock.com, 20; © Nastya81/Dreamstime.com, 22; © HUBERT YANN/iStockphoto, 24; © scubaluna/iStockphoto, 24; © Song Heming/Dreamstime.com, 24; © Orlandin/Dreamstime.com, 25; © Aneese/Thinkstock, 26; © Julian W/Shutterstock.com, 26; © Juniors Bildarchiv GmbH / Alamy Stock Photo, 27; © Frances van der Merwe/Shutterstock.com, 28; © inkwelldodo/Shutterstock.com, 28; © Andrey Pavlov/Thinkstock, 28; © Steven Ellingson/Shutterstock.com, 29; © Szasz-Fabian Jozsef/Shutterstock.com, 30; © 4loops/iStockphoto, 31

Graphic Element Credits: ©tukkki/Shutterstock.com, back cover, front cover, multiple interior pages; ©paprika/Shutterstock.com, back cover, front cover, multiple interior pages; ©Silhouette Lover/Shutterstock.com, multiple interior pages

45th Parallel Press is an imprint of Cherry Lake Publishing.

Library of Congress Cataloging-in-Publication Data

Names: Loh-Hagan, Virginia, author. | Loh-Hagan, Virginia. Wild wicked wonderful.
Title: Top 10 : partnerships / by Virginia Loh-Hagan.
Other titles: Top ten partnerships
Description: Ann Arbor, Michigan : Cherry Lake Publishing, [2017] | Series:
    Wild wicked wonderful | Includes index.
Identifiers: LCCN 2016029719| ISBN 9781634721394 (hardcover) | ISBN 9781634722711 (pbk.) |
    ISBN 9781634722056 (pdf) | ISBN 9781634723374 ebook)
Subjects: LCSH: Mutualism (Biology)–Juvenile literature. | Animal behavior–Juvenile literature. |
    Animals–Miscellanea–Juvenile literature.
Classification: LCC QH548.3 .L64 2017 | DDC 577.8/52–dc23
LC record available at https://lccn.loc.gov/2016029719

Printed in the United States of America
Corporate Graphics

About the Author

Dr. Virginia Loh-Hagan is an author, university professor, former classroom teacher, and curriculum designer. She lives in San Diego and has an extreme partnership with her very tall husband and very naughty dogs. To learn more about her, visit www.virginialoh.com.

TABLE OF CONTENTS

INTRODUCTION

Animals team up. They work together. They hunt together. They defend each other.

Animal partners need each other to survive. They depend on each other. They **benefit** from their partnership. Benefit means to get something good.

Some animals have extreme partnerships. They're nature's odd couples. Some animal partnerships are odder than others. These are the most exciting partnerships in the animal world!

Animals worry about getting eaten. They need to be brave.

chapter one

GECKOS

Geckos climb walls. They climb steep cliffs. They climb ceilings. They hang upside down. They dare to climb anything.

They have amazing sticky toes. They cling to surfaces. They quickly run up. They stick and unstick their feet. They do this 15 times a second.

Their feet have tiny **ridges**. Ridges are raised marks. Their feet have tiny hairs. These hairs have split ends. There are more than 150,000 hairs. Their tiny hairs bond with the surface. Each hair grips the surface. All the hairs together

Unlike other climbing animals, geckos just use their toes to climb.

create a tight hold. This is how they stick to things. They have super climbing powers.

Chapter two

SLOTHS

Sloths live in jungles. They live in South America. They dare to spend their lives upside down. They hang by their fingernails. They have special claws. Their claws are long and curved. They have strong grips. They don't fall down. They even stay hanging after death.

Their bodies are made for hanging. Their organs are upside down. They can't walk upright on the ground. Their bodies can't pump blood to the head. They'd feel great pain. Most animals can't hang like sloths.

Sloths have unique hair. It grows from their bellies to their backs.

Sloths have long tongues. Their tongues stick out 12 inches (30.5 centimeters). They can grab things out of their reach. They can turn their heads almost all the way around.

chapter three
ORANGUTANS

Orangutans are part of the great apes family. They're four times stronger than humans. They live on Southeast Asian islands. They live in tall trees. They sleep in trees. They build nests. They use branches and leaves. They're the largest animals to live in trees.

Orangutans dare to swing through these trees. They have no safety nets. They don't worry about falling. They swing to eat. They swing to avoid danger on the ground.

Their bodies are made to swing. They have **flexible** hips. Flexible means they can move easily. Their feet are like

An adult male orangutan can weigh as much as an adult human.

hands. They can grip easily. They have large arm spans.
Males can stretch their arms 7 feet (2 meters).

Orangutans take risks. Seven out of 10 adult orangutans break arms or legs.

Orangutans are very smart. They use tools. They use sticks to get honey and bugs. They use leaves as umbrellas. They use leaves as toilet paper. They use branches to scratch their back. They can pick locks.

They talk to each other. They move through the forests. They make a lot of noise. They howl. They can be heard 1.2 miles (2 kilometers) away. They stay out of each other's way.

HUMANS DO WHAT?!?

Humans do daring things for fun. They push limits. They want to be like animals. Humans want to fly. Felix Baumgartner flew. He dived down from space. He jumped from a special balloon. It had a small spaceship underneath it. He was more than 128,000 feet (39 km) above Earth. He tumbled in the free fall. But he saved himself. He jumped from 24 miles above Earth. This is the longest and highest free fall. Humans also want to climb. Alexander Rusinov is called the Russian Spider-Man. He climbs high walls. He jumps between rooftops. He does handstands on the edge of skyscrapers and bridges. He hangs from tall buildings. One of his most extreme stunts is dangling one-handed off construction equipment. Pictures show him dangling with one hand. He is giving the thumbs-up signal with the other hand. He dangles from hundreds of feet in the air. He doesn't use safety wires.

chapter four

TREE SNAKES

Asian tree snakes move through Asian rainforests. They have an extreme way of moving. They dare to climb without arms and legs.

They climb steep surfaces. They climb tall trees. They push against the rough edges of bark. They have scales on their bellies. They use their bellies to climb up.

They fly across treetops. They suck in their bellies. This forms a **parachute**. A parachute looks like the top of a balloon. The snakes' bellies catch the air. They get pushed

Tree snakes fall from high places.
They crash-land on their bellies.

forward. This helps them glide from tree to tree. They don't really land. They crash. Their bellies flop against the tree.

chapter five

AFRICAN CROWNED EAGLES

African crowned eagles are large birds of **prey**. Prey are animals that are hunted for food. These eagles are powerful. They can kill prey over four times bigger than them. They have thick, strong legs. They have large **talons**. The talons are on each toe. They're sharp, curved claws. They're long and strong. Eagles use talons to catch prey. Talons can break spines and crush skulls.

They have daring flying skills. They're built for flying among trees. Their wings are short and wide. They have long tails. They fly easily through branches. They can also fly straight up.

African crowned eagles surprise their prey.

Eagles stay still to hunt. They sit in a tree. They watch for prey. Then they drop down onto their prey. They attack.

Chapter six

BROWN PELICANS

Brown pelicans fly high above the coast line. They fly over the Atlantic and Pacific Oceans. They love fish. They land on water. They lunge at the fish. But they also want to catch deeper fish. They developed an extreme hunting move.

They are daring divers. They dive from high in the sky. They fold back their wings. They open special air **sacs**. Sacs are like bags. The air sacs are under their skin. This takes in the shock.

They hit the water hard. They have a lot of force. They travel 40 miles (64 km) per hour. They surprise the fish. They catch fish 6 feet (1.8 m) below the surface.

chapter seven

CLICK BEETLES

Click beetles jump at daring speeds. They jump without using their legs. They put up with more **g-forces** than any other animal. G-forces are a result of speed or gravity. These forces pull on objects as they fall. They strain objects.

Bugs roll on their backs. They try to roll over. They use their feet. Click beetles are different. They have a tiny peg on their bellies. They flex their muscles. They arch their backs. They release the peg. This makes a loud click. They shoot themselves into the air.

Click beetles launch themselves to move.

They can reach 400 **g**'s. (A "g" is one unit of a g-force.)
This is 80 times more than a human cannonball.

Click beetles launch higher than their body length. They tumble several times in the air.

Click beetles fling themselves into the air. They do this to right themselves. They also do this to protect themselves. They create a lot of force. They can escape from **predators**. Predators are hunters.

They tumble into the air. They have a 50 percent chance of landing on their feet. So they may need to jump several times.

Sometimes, clicking doesn't work. There are still predators around. They tuck in their legs. They pretend to be dead.

They don't need safety nets. They have hard shells. Their tough shells protect them.

DID YOU KNOW...?

- Beetles have been around since Jurassic times. There are about 350,000 species of beetles. They survived because they adapted.

- Inventors created climbing tools. They studied sticky forces. They were inspired by gecko feet. The hairs on gecko feet are called setae.

- Weddell seals sleep. They rest. They may remain in the same spot. They lay down for hours. They melt a hole in the ice. They use their own body heat.

- Bharals have very strange horns. They grow upward. Then they grow out to the side. Then they point backward. Males have longer horns than females. Horns can grow up to 31.5 inches (80 cm) long.

- Sloths digest food slowly. They only need to use the bathroom once a week. They do this on the ground.

- Flying snakes are better gliders than flying squirrels.

- Arctic foxes wait for the baby barnacle geese to fall. They eat the dead or injured babies.

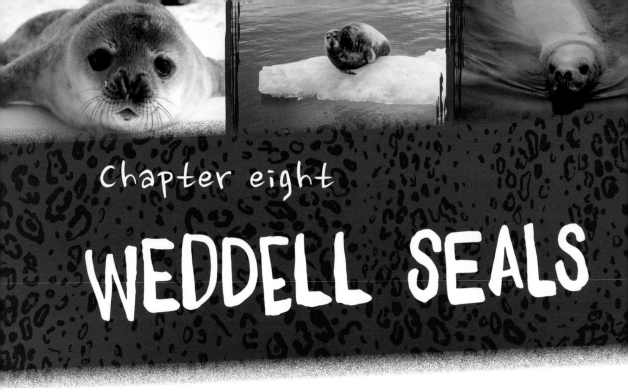

Chapter eight

WEDDELL SEALS

Weddell seals live in Antarctica. No other **mammal** lives farther south than these seals. Mammals are warm-blooded. They have hair or fur. They give birth to live young. They feed their young milk.

They dare to live in freezing waters. They swim under the ice. They have a thick layer of **blubber**. Blubber is fat. It keeps them warm.

They must surface to breath. They use their teeth. They scrape the ice. They make airholes. They have to keep these holes from freezing over. They have to know where their

Weddell seals can find breathing holes even after an hour of swimming.

holes are. They have **sonar**. Sonar is the ability to find things by using sound. They make strange calls. They listen for echoes. They find their way back to their holes.

Many Weddell seals wear down their teeth.

Weddell seals are daring divers. They dive down more than 2,000 feet (609.6 m). The seals can **collapse** their lungs. They close their lungs. This saves air. They have extra oxygen in their blood and muscles.

They can hold their breath. They can swim for about 80 minutes. They're fast divers. They dive more than 394 feet (120 m) per minute.

They dive to find food. They mainly hunt at night. They have great eyesight.

Baby Weddell seals swim at about two weeks old. Mothers push them in.

When Animals Attack!

Paul Rosolie dared a green anaconda to eat him. It's one of the largest snakes in the world. It captures prey. It eats large animals like jaguars, deer, and pigs. It squeezes prey to death. It swallows prey whole. Rosolie found a 20-foot-long (6 m) anaconda. He was in South America. He wore a black suit made of metal. The suit protected him against teeth and the anaconda's stomach acid. He put pig's blood on him. He crawled toward the anaconda. The anaconda tried to escape. Rosolie provoked it. So, it pounced. It coiled itself around Rosolie's body. It clamped its jaws on his head. Rosolie felt his arm breaking. Part of his head was in the anaconda's mouth. He asked his team to rescue him. The team got him out. Rosolie did this for a television show. He wanted to raise money. The money would help protect the anaconda's home.

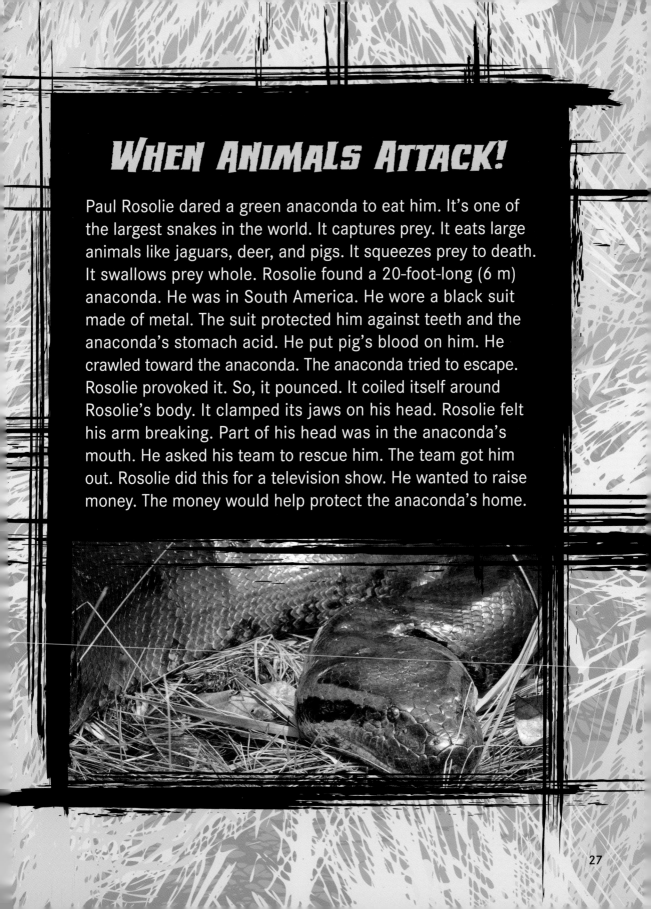

chapter nine
BHARALS

Bharals are mountain sheep. They live 14,000 feet (4,267 m) above ground. They live in the Himalayan Mountains. These are the highest mountains in the world. They're in Asia.

Bharals are daring climbers. They have flexible **hooves**. Hooves are the hard part that covers the foot of an animal. Their front toes are split. They have rubbery pads. They grip the rocks. Their pointed toenails fit into tiny cracks. They climb mountain edges. They climb steep mountains.

They take great risks. Only half of the bharals survive their first year. Many are killed by falling rocks. They're killed by

As part of the mating ritual, males try to knock each other off a cliff.

avalanches. Avalanches are falling walls of snow. But bharals are safer on the cliffs than on the ground. Predators can eat them on the ground.

chapter ten
BABY BARNACLE GEESE

Barnacle geese live in the Arctic. They nest at the top of high cliffs. They're about 300 feet (91.4 m) above ground. They're far away from predators. But they're also far away from food.

Baby barnacle geese can't fly. They can barely walk. But, at three days old, they are daring **BASE jumpers**. BASE jumpers jump from high places. They jump off objects.

To leave the nest the baby barnacle geese step off the cliff. They fall. They can't fly. They have a fluffy down coat. This helps them float. They have a 50 percent chance of

Baby barnacle geese free-fall from a cliff.

living. The cliffs are high. Animals want to eat them. If they live, they travel with their parents.

CONSIDER THIS!

TAKE A POSITION! Some animals are built to be daredevils. Humans have to invent tools to help them be daredevils. What are some examples of this? Do you think humans should be daredevils? Argue your point with reasons and evidence.

SAY WHAT? Learn more about human daredevils. Explain the differences and similarities between human daredevils and animal daredevils.

THINK ABOUT IT! Some animals are in danger of losing their homes and ways of life. For example, humans are destroying rainforests. This affects several animals in this book. What do you think about this issue?

LEARN MORE!

- Davies, Nicola, and Neal Layton (illustrator). *Extreme Animals: The Toughest Creatures on Earth*. Cambridge, MA: Candlewick, 2009.
- "Ultimate Animal Countdown: Daredevils," National Geographic Wild, http://channel. nationalgeographic.com/wild/ultimate-animal-countdown/episodes/daredevils1/.

GLOSSARY

avalanches (AV-uh-lanch-iz) walls of snow flowing down a mountain

BASE jumpers (BASE JUHMP-urz) people or animals who jump off objects from high places

blubber (BLUHB-ur) fat

collapse (kuh-LAPS) close or cave in

daredevils (DAIR-dev-uhlz) people or animals who do dangerous things

feats (FEETS) accomplishments, actions

flexible (FLEK-suh-buhl) easy to move

g (JEE) unit of g-force

g-forces (JEE FORS-ez) gravity forces as a result of speed or gravity

hooves (HOOVZ) the hard part that covers the foot of an animal

mammal (MAM-uhl) warm-blooded animal that has hair or fur, has live births, and feeds milk to their young

parachute (PA-ruh-shoot) safety device that helps people glide or fall

predators (PRED-uh-turz) hunters

prey (PRAY) animals that are hunted

ridges (RIJ-iz) raised marks

sacs (SAKS) bags

sonar (SOH-nahr) the ability to find things by using sound

survive (sur-VIVE) to live

talons (TAL-uhnz) long, sharp, curved claws on birds

INDEX